Putin's Ally Dead In DC

Can the official explanation be believed?

William Dunkerley

Copyright © 2017 by William Dunkerley

ALL RIGHTS RESERVED

No part of this publication may be reproduced in any way without the prior express written consent of the copyright owner.

Published by
Omnicom Press
New Britain, CT, USA
Publishers since 1981

www.OmnicomPress.com

ISBN-13: 978-1979535502
ISBN-10: 1979535507
Printed in the United States of America

Putin's Ally Dead in DC is part of the "Russia: Straight Talk on Hushed Issues" monograph series. It is dedicated to the concept of a safe, sustaining, and positive relationship between the United States and the Russian Federation.

A list of other monographs in this series can be found at:

www.OmnicomPress.com/monographs

CONTENTS

Chapter 1
THE MEDIA MOBSTER

"You walked into the party / Like you were walking onto a yacht." Those lines from Carly Simon's *You're So Vain* classic song flashed through my mind as I watched a somewhat gaudy-looking middle aged fellow enter a large meeting room at a big media confab in New York City.

He was affluently decked out in a dark, very expensive suit, French cuffs and all, wearing a lot of gold jewelry. Right behind him was a tall, drop-dead beautiful assistant who was hanging on his every word. "What's this Russian mafia guy doing here?" I wondered to myself.

Well, it turned out he was not a Brighton Beach mobster; he was Putin's media minister. He was there to deliver a talk on press freedom in Russia.

I casually nodded hello to him.

His name was Mikhail Lesin. And before the proceedings got started, the government minister and his assistant huddled around his mobile phone, deep in conversation with someone. Then they abruptly left. No explanation. The meeting went on without Lesin.

That was back in the early days of Putin's tenure in Moscow. And as it came to pass, this puzzling "mobster" episode was just one act in the mystery surrounding the life of Mikhail Lesin.

The final act was his 2015 mysterious death in a Washington DC hotel room. It's still not clear what really happened to him. At one point reports were intimating that he bludgeoned himself to death. Can you believe that?

Chapter 2
WHO'S LESIN?

Before becoming a member of Putin's cabinet, Mikhail Lesin had already made his mark in the Russian media field. He founded a company called Video International, later named Vi. Exactly when it started operations is discrepantly reported. Bloomberg pegs it as 1987. Others claim it was in the early 1990s. But whenever it started, the company would eventually gain near-monopoly status in the media advertising business.

What did Vi actually do? A major activity was to act as an advertising middleman between struggling Russian media companies and fledgling advertisers in the wild media market of the brand new Russian Federation.

Vi filled a need. Media company staffs lacked the

business acumen for effectively selling advertising space or time. These were people who largely came out of Soviet editorial offices. They were editors; business wasn't their game. So they gladly allowed in a middleman who would make the sales, collect the money, and share it with them. It seemed like a good deal. For the advertisers, Vi gave them an opportunity to deal with sales people who actually understood the advertising game, and could strike up special deals that benefited the advertisers. In all it was a very crafty venture that commanded considerable influence over the dependent media outlets.

During Yeltsin's Time

In 1996, when Boris Yeltsin stood for reelection, Lesin pitched in to help. It was quite a challenge, given Yeltsin's unpopularity in Russia. In the end he won reelection, despite going into the campaign season with only low single digit approval ratings. A lot of people take credit for that sleight-of-hand miracle. Lesin is often named as having been one of the top strategists.

And so when Vladimir Putin became prime minister (and a presumed presidential heir apparent), he threw out the well-respected and dedicated media minister Ivan Laptev and replaced him with Lesin. Laptev was quite unhappy over that and in private conversation told me in no polite language what he thought of how Putin treated him.

Lesin's New Agenda

As Lesin took charge he espoused many constructive plans to reform Russia's dysfunctional media sector. I was flattered that on several occasions he even paraphrased analyses I had presented in speeches and in print about the development trajectory that was needed. To my chagrin, however, he was not quick on the implementation.

At the start of 2001, writing in Sreda, Russia's first professional magazine for media managers, I remarked: "In the past, criticism of Minister Lesin has ranged from calling him a mindless patsy for those who want to stifle the press, to a cunning shill in the government for his own business interests. Now, he has positioned himself as an advocate of 'level and healthy competition.' Will he follow through on that?"

I had my doubts. Later that year I sought an invitation from the Putin administration to analyze the media sector and make recommendations for improvement. Soon a letter came asking me and my associates to do just that. Interestingly, it came direct from Lesin's ministry. The letter promised to share my findings widely within the administration..

After submitting my report, its recommendations were largely implemented and incorporated into law. The benefits of this new deal, lamentably, were never significantly realized. But that's a long story, one that's detailed in my book *Medvedev's Media Affairs*.

Stepping Down

Lesin left Putin's cabinet around the time the president's first four year term ended. Although I had been sometimes critical of his work as minister, I thought things took a turn for the worse after his departure. Perhaps he deserved more credit than what he had received.

Not a lot was heard from Lesin following his retirement from Putin's cabinet. He became relatively low-key. Nonetheless, during this period he founded Russia Today (now RT) and was head of the Gazprom media empire. He left that post at the tail end of 2014 innocuously citing family reasons.

Less than a year later Lesin was back at the top

of the news. World headlines announced that Putin's ally was found dead in Washington DC.

In the aftermath of that I filed several reports that now constitute the following chapters.

Chapter 3
A MYSTERIOUS DEATH

Filed: November 11, 2015

US Attacks RT, Now Its Founder Discovered Dead in DC. Is this another round in the ongoing tit-for-tat conflict between Russia and the US?

RT founder Mikhail Lesin is dead at 57. Both RT (formerly Russia Today) and Lesin himself have been the subjects of bitter US attacks in recent times.

Lesin's body was discovered on Friday, November 6 in a Washington DC hotel. As of this writing no official cause of death has been publically reported.

Lesin is widely credited with being the force behind the founding of RT, the controversial international broadcaster supported by the Russian government.

Just days before Lesin was found dead, RT was the target of a sharp attack at a US Senate hearing. In testimony, American Enterprise Institute scholar Leon Aron asserted that the aim of RT is "to devalue the notions of democratic transparency and accountability, to undermine confidence in objective reporting, and to litter the news with half-truths." They were very strong words. Aron didn't explain how he became privy to RT's covert aims.

McCain's Rant

Even stronger repudiation has come from the McCain Institute. It said that "RT is the key to Putin's propaganda effort to discredit the West and obfuscate the truth of Russian actions." McCain claims, "It is time for the democratic community of nations to go on the offensive."

"Freeze the assets of Putin's state-funded RT cable network" is the battle plan advocated by the McCain organization. Apparently McCain would like to put an end to RT. That's some concept for a "democratic community of nations," isn't it? The vaunted American ideal of free speech and a free press seems to go out the window for McCain when it comes to RT. So much for allowing citizens to separate fact from fiction for themselves.

Upping the Pressure

The attack on Lesin focused on his personal financial affairs. In 2014 Mississippi senator Roger Wicker called upon federal authorities to investigate whether Lesin had used what Radio Liberty called "dirty money" to purchase expensive California real estate.

Were Lesin's financial affairs not on the up-and-up? I don't know. But it seems curious that Wicker wanted to take this on. His state is Mississippi, not California. Isn't it really odd that he would choose to single out Lesin for special treatment?

I sought clarification with multiple calls to Wicker's press secretary. I left messages explaining the issue I was calling about. But there was no return call. I had hit a brick wall.

Wicker's call to investigate Lesin came in the form of a July 29, 2014 letter to then US Attorney General Eric Holder. In it Wicker questioned the legitimacy of Lesin's personal wealth. He cited the California real estate purchases among other concerns. Wicker wrote, "That a Russian public servant could have amassed the considerable funds required to acquire and maintain these assets in Europe and the United States raises serious questions."

It seems Wicker was trying to mislead the Attorney General into believing that Lesin's only legitimate income came from a paltry government salary.

It's well known that Lesin was a co-founder of a Russian company called Video International that operates in the advertising field. Today the company (now renamed Vi) has 2000 employees in three countries and has over $2 billion in annual revenues, according to the company's website.

How much did Lesin get out of all this? It's hard to tell. And it's unclear how he juggled his Vi role with duties as Putin's media minister from 1999 to 2004. Observers used to joke that Lesin was the Minister of his own business interests.

Wacky Wicker

Ironically, Wicker contradicted his own aspersion that Lesin was living above his visible means. He admitted to Holder that Lesin had been "director general of Gazprom Media Holding, Russia's largest media group." Surely he was well compensated for that work.

It does not take much research to find that Lesin was not simply a public servant receiving a regular pay check.

Even back in November 2000 a UPI story said, "His personal wealth was estimated by ex-Prime Minister Yevgeny Primakov at in excess of $180 million." And that was at a much earlier point in Lesin's career.

It's quite a mystery why Wicker tried to hoodwink Holder. What was Wicker's game? What or who motivated him to play it?

Lesin Was No Angel

I'm certainly not claiming that Lesin was a model businessman through all this.

Even the Russian news agency Sputnik had this to say: "To be sure, Lesin was not without his sins, and was involved in the dirty media games of late 90s Russia."

The news coverage of Lesin's death has tied him closely to Putin. Some of the headlines included:

"Putin Media Henchman Found Dead in Washington Hotel" —*The New Indian Express*

"Death of Putin Ally Mikhail Lesin Sparks Conspiracy Theories" —*FT*

"Russian Media Censor Dies of Heart Attack in Washington's Dupont Circle" —*Kyiv Post*

One *Kyiv Post* commenter said, "Strange he was a civil servant [and] acquired 28 million dollars worth of real estate in Los Angeles, California, USA, as well as much more across Europe and the US." It seems the specious information in the Lesin death story is easily believed by unsuspecting audiences.

What about the Yeltsin Connection?

I didn't see much media mention that Lesin had played a role in the Yeltsin administration.

According to Lenta.ru, he was a key player in the 1996 reelection of Boris Yeltsin. That was a contest Yeltsin had entered with only about a five percent approval rating.

Following the election victory Lesin became Yeltsin's head of PR. Toward the end of Yeltsin's tenure he headed a project to consolidate all state owned media properties.

Now Lesin's death leaves open several mysteries: How did he die? Why did Senator Wicker make material misrepresentations to the US Attorney General to spark an investigation of Lesin? Why did the Western media focus on Lesin's role with Putin and RT to the exclusion of his involvement in the Yeltsin era?

I think if Wicker were to come clean and explain himself, we might be able to start putting Lesin's final years into a clearer perspective.

Chapter 4
A COVER-UP UNDERWAY?

Filed: December 16, 2015

*Putin Ally Dead in DC Buried in LA -- Police
Mum on Details. In the absence of answers,
rumors fly wildly about.*

Suspicions surrounding the unexplained death of
Putin ally Mikhail Lesin are persisting
unabatedly. A *New York Times* December 14
piece added to the enigma. "A Mansion, a Shell
Company, and Resentment in Bel Air" in part
casts aspersions about Lesin's real estate holdings
in California.

A former media minister and advisor to Putin,
Lesin was found dead in a Washington DC hotel
room in early November. To date, the police have
not been forthcoming with any real explanation

of what happened.

Meanwhile rumors swirl about in the absence of an official ruling. They include reports that he did not die but was put into an identity protection program, that his death involved a homosexual assignation, and that he was murdered on Kremlin orders.

I've seen no evidence to support any of those rumors. And when I asked the police about them, they declined comment.

In the News

Some news accounts say that Lesin had moved his family to California. If that's the case, it probably explains why he was buried there.

Media reporting on all this, however, has been pretty questionable, even down to basic details. For instance, the *Moscow Times* reported his body was discovered in a "comparatively un-luxurious" DC hotel. But the *Irish Times* claims "Lesin was found in a luxury suite." I suppose that one man's dump can be another's castle. The Irish story added that the hotel is "Irish owned." Maybe that has something to do with the differing perceptions. The hotel "is close to many of the main embassies in Washington, the *Irish*

Times pridefully added.

But the booby prize for journalistic performance has to go to *Ukraine Today*. It ran a report by journalist Vitaly Portnikov titled, "The Monster Is Dead: How Mikhail Lesin managed to kill Russian journalism." Extolling the superiority of Russian journalism in the 1990s compared to that in Ukraine, Portnikov boasted, "The reports were professional. Everything was according to standards. Can anyone of sound mind say that today Russian journalism is an example of anything but dishonesty and disregard for these standards?" he asked.

Journalistic Misunderstanding

Maybe Portnikov thinks I'm nuts, but he seems to have just a superficial understanding of Russia's journalistic scene.

There were no standards back in the day. Yeltsin era laws made it practically impossible for media companies to operate independently and profitably. That sent the outlets straight into the arms of oligarchs and government officials. They were willing to foot the bill in return for the opportunity to color the news in their own favor. Disseminating news content that is biased by the wishes of a financial client whether private or political isn't freedom of the press. It's commercialized dishonesty.

My Own Observations

As a media business analyst and consultant I've done intensive work in seventeen different Russian cities. I'm quite familiar with the situation on the ground then and now. It surely doesn't match Portnikov's effusive-cum-condemnatory nonsense. I detail the real media milieu in my book *Medvedev's Media Affairs*.

The truth is that during Lesin's tenure great strides were made in establishing for the first time a regulatory environment that would permit the successful operation of independent media companies. He lamented the prevalence of "illegal revenues from unregistered, indirect advertising." It is a shame that "articles are ordered and paid for, and written in someone's interest," he added. Russians so resented that kind of journalism that in survey-after-survey a vast majority called for the reinstitution of some kind of censorship. And that's perhaps what they got as the Kremlin took various key media properties under its wing.

Many Lesin case observers find drama in the long time it's taking for the police to disclose what happened to him. Some media bemoan a police suggestion that details may not be released until sometime in February. But experts in the field who I talked with explain that's within normal and routine standards. So there's not necessarily any reason for suspicion there. That means the police have a right to be mum, at least for the time being.

Chapter 5
BLUDGEONED TO DEATH?

Filed: March 11, 2016

FLASH: Blow to Head Killed Putin ex-Media Boss in DC. The mystery just took a dramatic turn.

Former Russian press minister and Putin advisor Mikhail Lesin's death in a DC hotel has now been ruled a result of blunt force trauma to his head.

Mysteriously, the coroner's ruling has just been released on the November 5, 2015 death. According to the coroner, "blunt force injuries of the neck, torso, upper extremities and lower extremities" were also found.

Now the main point of mystery turns to why

news of these obvious physical injuries was
suppressed by DC officials for over four months.

Earlier news stories had attributed Lesin's death
to a heart attack. It's perplexing how death of the
badly beaten Lesin could have been presumed
the result of an internal body malfunction.

Chapter 6
MALICIOUS FABRICATIONS

Filed: November 1, 2016

Putin Foes Caught in Malicious Fabrications about Kremlin Insider Lesin's Death. Coroner's final decision reveals all.

A US Senator and a Russian opposition figure are among those who have tripped themselves up with their fabrications about Mikhail Lesin's 2015 death. Lesin was a former Russian media advertising tycoon, state media minister, and later head of the Gazprom-Media holding company. He died in Washington DC amid circumstances that went unexplained fully until October 28 of this year.

What did Putin's foes first have to say about Lesin's death?

Russian opposition figure and Putin foe Alexei Nevalny had a lot to say. On March 13, 2016 the *Independent* ran the headline: "Mikhail Lesin death: Vladimir Putin's propaganda chief reportedly flew out of LA 40 days after his death." The story claims Alexei Navalny, a Putin opposition leader, said the incident "smells of a witness protection programme." The *Daily Mail* reported that Navalny claimed to have proof.

Was Lesin's reported demise just a cover-up?

But a month later, Navalny seemed to have backed away from that allegation. According to the Voice of America "Navalny said he had no 'proof' or definitive evidence, but indicated that Lesin may have died because, 'as they say in detective stories, he knew too much.'"

So Navalny had come to believe that Lesin was indeed dead after all. But now Navalny intimated that perhaps Putin was to blame.

While making a case to VOA that Putin is corrupt, Navalny said he was convinced "that Lesin knew a lot. Not just about corruption in the highest echelons of power, but [he] was one of the organizers of a corruption scheme in which Putin himself was personally complicit. And against the backdrop of his death, against the

backdrop of the strange things that were
happening around him, it's a more than
reasonable assumption that, in any contacts he
may have had with the federal authorities in the
United States, Lesin may have been asked about
it."

Navalny Wasn't Alone

Other theories in the news claimed:

--Lesin's death was connected with his alleged
role as a CIA informer.
--His demise was related to a secret romantic
tryst gone wrong.
--Lesin's body was cremated to destroy evidence
of what really happened.

Many of the news reports mentioned Mississippi
Senator Roger Wicker who considered Lesin to
be a very suspicious character. He very well may
have been. Once while having lunch with Ivan
Laptev, Lesin's ministerial predecessor, I joked
about when I saw Lesin at a New York meeting
in the early 2000s. I first mistook him for some
kind of Russian mafia guy, just based on how he
was dressed and the gorgeous gun-moll looking
young lady that accompanied him.

In July 2014 Wicker seemed to have more

serious concerns. He was moved to tip off the US Attorney General. It wasn't based on Lesin's appearance. Wicker had become aware that Lesin owned expensive residential property in California. He believed that meant something sinister was afoot. Wicker said about Lesin, "He acquired multiple residences at a cost of over $28 million."

"That a Russian public servant could have amassed the considerable funds required to acquire and maintain these assets in ... the United States raises serious questions," Wicker told ABC News.

And Putin?

Wicker wasn't fond of Putin either. In March 2014 he had written an article for the *Washington Examiner* titled, "Hillary Clinton was right about Vladimir Putin and Adolf Hitler the first time." Clinton has been quoted many times likening Putin to Hitler.

Wicker was and is a member of the Senate Armed Forces Committee. I find it very disturbing that a member of that influential committee could be espousing ideas so distant from reality as these. A simple google search could have told him that Lesin was no simple government service worker pulling down a measly salary. Lesin's Video International business had a near-monopoly grip on the media advertising business in Russia years ago. In fact when he was Putin's media minister, many critics mused that he was the Minister of his own business.

Was Wicker's research so lame that he knew nothing of Lesin other than his role in the Russian bureaucracy? Was he that stupid? Or is there something sinister about Wicker's interest in Lesin? I don't know whether there is or isn't. But the incongruity of his factless demonization of Putin, and Wicker's seemingly malicious letter to the Attorney General about Lesin, throw up a red flag.

Maybe the Attorney General should look into Wicker's business dealings to see if something fishy is going on there.

What Really Happened?

So what's the truth about Lesin's death?

The final police account is that he was dead drunk in his hotel room, fell multiple times, injuring his lower and upper torso, and inflicted a fatal blow to his head.

I don't know whether that is the honest truth or
not.

But if we are to believe people like Navalny and
Wicker it would seem that the Washington
coroner is in the bag for Putin.

Wow, what a Russian conspiracy that would be!

Appendix I
THE AUTHOR

William Dunkerley is a media business analyst
and Senior Fellow at American University in
Moscow. He has worked on behalf of US
interests in promoting press freedom in Eastern
Europe and the former Soviet Union. He was
commissioned by the International Federation of
Journalists to analyze problems in certain
Western press coverage of Russian issues. Mr.
Dunkerley has been instrumental in shaping laws
governing the media in Eastern Europe and
Russia and has offered testimony to the United
States Congress on media concerns. He has
personally done intensive work in seven post
communist countries, including interventions in
seventeen different cities across all Russia. He is
principal of William Dunkerley Publishing
Consultants, and publisher of two industry
monthlies, *Editors Only* and the *STRAT* newsletter.

Appendix II
THIS SERIES

"Russia: Straight Talk on Hushed Issues" is a
monograph series that looks behind the popular
headlines and presents iconoclastic analyses. The
books explain aspects of mainstream news that are
either being distorted, glossed over, or hushed up.

The etiology of these media distortions is
complex. Historically there was little harshness in
the coverage of Yeltsin's misdeeds, perhaps a
result of Western giddiness over the collapse of
the Soviet Union.

When Putin entered the scene in 1999 the kid
gloves came off. He was demonized. Russian
tycoons who had been involved in skullduggery
under Yeltsin found the new leader problematic.

Boris Berezovsky, one of the tycoons, carried

media attacks to new heights after fleeing to London in 2001 to evade corruption charges. He packaged and distributed highly engaging news stories with associated graphics and interview opportunities to media outlets worldwide. Probably because of that convenience, they were readily accepted by the media unquestioningly despite their lack of factual bases.

Inexplicably, after Berezovsky's 2014 death, the stream of demonizing stories continued. Had Berezovsky's campaign just made an indelible impression that still taints the views of media and political leaders in the US and elsewhere? Or is there a new kingpin yet to be identified?

Regardless, many people have indeed formed beliefs based on the prevalence of distorted news and are committed to them. It would be unrealistic to think many of these folks will accept any contravening facts and analyses.

So the intention of this series is to give open-minded audiences in the US and other Western countries insights into misleading and fabricated reportage. That should allow them to arrive at more realistic and fact-based understandings, thus facilitating their serving more responsibly as members of our society. The intention is not to exonerate anyone who has been accused, but to point out that the accusers are liars and fabricators. (Note: Monographs in this series appear in no particular order.)

H.G. Wells once said: "Civilization is in a race between education and catastrophe."

But what is now unfolding in the theater of US-Russia relations is a race between catastrophe and utter disaster.

One entrant is the United States, and the other is Russia. Which country is on which side actually makes no difference. In this race, there are allegations, then sanctions, and then retributions for the previous actions. It is a self perpetuating loop.

This is a race in which the winner will personify either political buffoonery or plain stupidity. And which of the two is the victor will also make no difference. The main point for the rest of us is that this race will cause us all to lose.

As part of the "Russia: Straight Talk on Hushed Issues" monograph series, this book is dedicated to ending that foolish race, and to the concept of a safe, sustaining, and positive relationship between the United States and the Russian Federation.

Appendix III
ACKNOWLEDGMENT

In the face of much media misinformation about Russia, I wish to acknowledge the effort and perseverance of all who have spoken and written the honest truth. They have shown great courage in bucking the unfortunate mainstream trend toward fabrication. Their work serves as an essential predicate to this book. --W.D.